A LifeGuide

THE MESSIAH

The Texts Behind Handel's Masterpiece

8 STUDIES FOR INDIVIDUALS OR GROUPS

Douglas Connelly

IVP Connect

An imprint of InterVarsity Press
Downers Grove, Illinois

InterVarsity Press
P.O. Box 1400, Downers Grove, IL 60515-1426
World Wide Web: www.ivpress.com
Email: email@ivpress.com

*InterVarsity Press® is the book-publishing division of InterVarsity Christian Fellowship/USA®, a
movement of students and faculty active on campus at hundreds of universities, colleges and schools
of nursing in the United States of America, and a member movement of the International Fellowship
of Evangelical Students. For information about local and regional activities, write Public Relations
Dept., InterVarsity Christian Fellowship/USA, 6400 Schroeder Rd., P.O. Box 7895, Madison, WI
53707-7895, or visit the IVCF website at <www.intervarsity.org>.*

LifeGuide® is a registered trademark of InterVarsity Christian Fellowship.

*All Scripture quotations, unless otherwise indicated, are taken from the Holy Bible, New
International Version®, NIV® Copyright © 1973, 1978, 1984, 2011 by Biblica, Inc.™ Used by
permission. All rights reserved worldwide.*

*While all stories in this book are true, some names and identifying information in this book have
been changed to protect the privacy of the individuals involved.*

Cover design: Cindy Kiple
Interior design: Beth Hagenberg
Cover image: © James Hearn/Dreamstime.com

ISBN 978-0-8308-3132-6

Printed in the United States of America ♾

g green
press
INITIATIVE

*As a member of the Green Press Initiative, InterVarsity Press is committed to
protecting the environment and to the responsible use of natural resources. To learn
more, visit greenpressinitiative.org.*

P	13	12	11	10	9	8	7	6	5	4	3	2	
Y	25	24	23	22	21	20	19	18	17	16	15	14	

Contents

Getting the Most
Out of *The Messiah*

Long before Jesus walked the hills of Galilee, the people of God were looking for a deliverer. Their expectations and hopes were shaped by passages of Scripture that spoke—sometimes clearly and sometimes in shadow—of a Redeemer, Anointed by God, who would restore to God's people all that had been lost to sin and rebellion and disobedience. At times, the prophets spoke in the language of a great king and a marvelous kingdom of peace. At other times, the promised One was described in terms of a humble servant who would suffer the penalty of human sin and loss.

When the New Testament witnesses began to tell the story of Jesus, they discovered that all the Old Testament passages about the Messiah found their fulfillment in this teacher from Nazareth. Almost every aspect of Jesus' life and ministry and death had been pictured long before in the writings of the prophets. Even the passages that described the promised One as a conquering King were fulfilled in the promises Jesus made about his glorious reign and future return. The early Christians could come to only one conclusion: Jesus of Nazareth was the promised Messiah.

This study guide will explore some of the key passages in the Old Testament about the Messiah and their completion in the life and saving work of Jesus. Each study will deepen your understanding and appreciation of who Jesus is. You will gain new insight into Jesus' character and power. You will see his whole career plotted out in the ancient writings of Israel.

These passages have had a profound effect on the imagination and worship of Christians for two thousand years. One of the greatest expressions of worship and adoration was written by George Handel. He called his oratorio *Messiah*. We hear it (or parts of it) sung every year during the Christmas season. What many listeners fail to realize is that the entire text of Handel's *Messiah* is drawn from Scripture—and it includes many of the Old Testament passages that shaped Israel's hope for their Redeemer.

So, while the focus of this study guide will be on the biblical passages about the coming Messiah, you will also have the option of exploring sections of Handel's adaptation of some of these passages in *Messiah*. I hope you will play a recording of the significant sections or sing those sections as part of your Bible study.

If you work through this study near the time of Advent or Easter, it will prepare your heart in a fresh way for those celebrations. But any time of the year, these studies will draw you closer to Jesus in adoration and appreciation. Be open to all that God desires to do in you as you take a long look at your Redeemer and Savior and King.

Suggestions for Individual Study

1. As you begin each study, pray that God will speak to you through his Word.

2. Read the introduction to the study and respond to the personal reflection question or exercise. This is designed to help you focus on God and on the theme of the study.

3. Each study deals with a particular passage so that you can delve into the author's meaning in that context. Read and reread the passage to be studied. The questions are written using the language of the New International Version, so you may wish to use that version of the Bible. The New Revised Standard Version is also recommended.

4. This is an inductive Bible study, designed to help you discover for yourself what Scripture is saying. The study includes three types of questions. Observation questions ask about the basic facts: who, what, when, where and how. Interpretation questions delve into the meaning of the passage. Application questions help you discover the implications of the text for growing in Christ. These three keys unlock the treasures of Scripture.

Write your answers to the questions in the spaces provided or in a personal journal. Writing can bring clarity and deeper understanding of yourself and of God's Word.

5. It might be good to have a Bible dictionary handy. Use it to look up any unfamiliar words, names or places.

6. Use the prayer suggestion to guide you in thanking God for what you have learned and to pray about the applications that have come to mind.

7. You may want to go on to the suggestion under "Now or Later," or you may want to use that idea for your next study.

Suggestions for Members of a Group Study

1. Come to the study prepared. Follow the suggestions for individual study mentioned above. You will find that careful preparation will greatly enrich your time spent in group discussion.

2. Be willing to participate in the discussion. The leader of your group will not be lecturing. Instead, he or she will be encouraging the members of the group to discuss what they have learned. The leader will be asking the questions that are found in this guide.

3. Stick to the topic being discussed. Your answers should be based on the verses which are the focus of the discussion and not on outside authorities such as commentaries or speakers. These studies focus on a particular passage of Scripture. Only rarely should you refer to other portions of the Bible. This allows for everyone to participate in in-depth study on equal ground.

4. Be sensitive to the other members of the group. Listen attentively when they describe what they have learned. You may be surprised by their insights! Each question assumes a variety of answers. Many questions do not have "right" answers, particularly questions that aim at meaning or application. Instead the questions push us to explore the passage more thoroughly.

When possible, link what you say to the comments of others. Also, be affirming whenever you can. This will encourage some of the more hesitant members of the group to participate.

5. Be careful not to dominate the discussion. We are sometimes so eager to express our thoughts that we leave too little opportunity for others to respond. By all means participate! But allow others to also.

6. Expect God to teach you through the passage being discussed and through the other members of the group. Pray that you will have an enjoyable and profitable time together, but also that as a result of the study you will find ways that you can take action individually and/or as a group.

7. Remember that anything said in the group is considered confidential and should not be discussed outside the group unless specific permission is given to do so.

8. If you are the group leader, you will find additional suggestions at the back of the guide.

1

His Name
Is Wonderful

Messiah's Character

We are all interested in names. Not long ago the world waited in anticipation to hear a royal baby's official name. We don't number our children; we name them. Names demonstrate our uniqueness and our personhood. One of the greatest compliments we can give another person is to call them by name.

Our names may link us to a grandparent or may be a favorite name chosen by our parents, but they don't have much significance beyond identifying us. That is not true with most biblical names—and especially with the names God gives to himself. God's names and titles reflect his character; they reveal what God is like.

GROUP DISCUSSION. Tell the group something about your name (or a nickname) and why you like or dislike your name.

PERSONAL REFLECTION. What name would God give you if he were to describe your character? What name would you give

God to describe your relationship or experience with him?

Seven hundred years before Jesus was born, the prophet Isaiah caught a glimpse of his amazing character. God's promised Messiah would be wonderful in every way! *Read Isaiah 9:6-7.*

1. What words and phrases in these verses point to this promised One as a human being?

What evidence do you find here that he is more than a human being?

2. When you need direction or counsel, who is the first person you turn to and why do you go to that person?

3. When and how do you turn to Jesus for direction and counsel—and how does he give that counsel to you?

4. What does it mean to you today that the "Mighty God" carries sovereign authority for our world on his shoulders?

5. Isaiah's title "Everlasting Father" can be translated "father of eternity" or "source of eternal things." In Jesus the eternal God was joined to human time and space. In what ways do those who follow Jesus find themselves linked to eternal blessings?

---

6. The Messiah would also bring *shalom*—not just the absence of conflict, but well-being or true peace in every area of life. Where in your life do you need to claim Jesus' offer of peace?

---

7. Which one of the four titles given to the Messiah in verse 6 fits Jesus best as you know him today?

Which title seems most distant from your experience and why?

---

8. How would you describe the scope and permanence of the Messiah's reign from these two verses?

---

9. In what ways does Jesus reign over your life, and how can you submit more fully to his lordship?

As you pray, submit yourself or some area of your life completely to Jesus. Let his peace enfold you.

Now or Later

George Frideric Handel's *Messiah* is a musical phenomenon. Every year this masterful piece is performed hundreds of times by everyone from well-rehearsed choirs with scores of voices to "join in where you can" community sing-alongs.

Handel's work belongs to the musical genre of oratorio. Like operas, oratorios are dramatic stories set entirely to music for soloists, choir or chorus, and orchestra. Unlike opera, oratorios do not include acting, costumes or stage scenery. Oratorios usually tell sacred stories drawn from the Bible or the lives of Christian saints.

Messiah is a combination of the music of Handel and the text compiled by Charles Jennings. Jennings drew every word from the Bible (sometimes the King James Version and sometimes from the translation used in the Book of Common Prayer).

The Old Testament writers promised that the coming of the Messiah would bring light into the darkness of a world shrouded in sin and death. In part 1, scene 3, section 2 of *Messiah*, darkness gives way to glorious light. The bass soloist sings a wandering melody, depicting our aimless journey in spiritual darkness. But then light begins to pierce the darkness.

The light is the virgin's child, Emmanuel. The scene reaches its climax in the coming of a Redeemer who will scatter the darkness with his presence and power—"for unto us a child is born."

Listen to both the aria ("The people that walked in darkness") and the chorus ("For unto us a child is born"). If you have access to the musical score, sing along with the soloist and the chorus. This is every Christian's story! We have seen the light in the face of Jesus.

2

The Virgin
Will Be with Child

Messiah's Birth

Instead of having children of their own, our son and daughter-in-law decided to welcome foster children into their home. They had already adopted one foster child, Joshua, when God brought a change of direction. At our Thanksgiving dinner one year, Kevin and Julie said that they had an announcement to make to the family—Julie was pregnant with their child. We all shouted and cried and laughed at the joyful news. When we met as a family a month later, the pregnant couple said they had another announcement to make. Their ultrasound images were labeled "Baby 1" and "Baby 2"—twins were on the way! This time the announcement was met with stunned silence and then shouts and laughter. Dakota and Autumn made their grand entrance the following May.

GROUP DISCUSSION. Tell a story about your birth or a joyous birth in your extended family. Why is a birth such a hope-filled event?

PERSONAL REFLECTION. What hopes and dreams did you have

for your children or other family members at their birth? Have you seen those dreams fulfilled?

Ahaz, the king of Judah, was shaking in his shoes. Enemy armies had gathered against him and the situation looked grim—until Isaiah, God's prophet, showed up! He gave Ahaz a sign that these enemies would not succeed against Judah. But Isaiah's words had a far greater significance than just resolving an ancient rivalry. He also spoke of a miraculous birth still to come that would change the course of humanity's story. *Read Isaiah 7:1-16.*

1. How would you describe the danger the land of Judah was in, and who was threatening God's people (vv. 1-6)?

2. What situations are you facing that are frightening or disruptive—and what forces are involved?

3. What assurance does God give to Ahaz through the prophet Isaiah (vv. 4, 7-9)?

What warning does Isaiah give (v. 9)?

4. When the Lord's prophet tells the king to ask for a sign that will confirm God's promise, the king refuses to ask for it. So God himself gives Ahaz a sign: a young woman (virgin) in Judah will conceive a child. Before the child is old enough to know right from wrong, what would happen to the nations plotting against Judah (vv. 14-16)?

5. If you were Ahaz, would you be comforted by or skeptical of this sign from God? Why?

Isaiah's words had a *historical* fulfillment in Isaiah's own day. Within a few months Judah's enemies had withdrawn from Judah. Within three years the kingdom of Israel was destroyed and within twelve years the nation of Aram was conquered—both by a much greater power, the empire of Assyria. But Isaiah's words had significance far beyond his own lifetime. As the writers of the New Testament looked back at Isaiah's prophecies, the Holy Spirit revealed a whole new level of meaning in Isaiah's words. There was also a *prophetic* fulfillment of these words in the birth of the promised Messiah seven hundred years after Isaiah spoke them. *Read Matthew 1:18-25.*

6. How would you describe Joseph's feelings toward Mary?

How would you describe Joseph's relationship with the Lord?

7. How did Matthew interpret Isaiah's "sign" (vv. 22-23)?

---

8. Jesus was conceived supernaturally in Mary, but he was born as a human baby. What is said in Isaiah's prophecy that makes you realize that Jesus is more than a human?

---

9. How have you experienced Jesus as "God with us"?

How can you bring comfort or encouragement to a friend with the truth that God is with us?

Meditate on Jesus as "God with us" over the next few days. In prayer, address Jesus as "Immanuel" or "God with us" to bring that reality more and more into your personal experience.

Now or Later

Isaiah's prophecy of a virgin conceiving a son is woven into part 1, scene 3, section 1 of Handel's *Messiah*. Isaiah's passage is spoken with minimal accompaniment. The great mystery of the virgin birth is announced with little fanfare. The alto's voice lends itself to that sense of awe—God is with us.

In response to the announcement comes a call to proclaim

good tidings to Zion—"thy light is come, and the glory of the Lord is risen upon thee."

Listen to all of part 1, scene 3, section 1—recitative (spoken), aria and chorus. Think about how God's light has broken into the darkness of your life. Meditate on the fact that by coming into our world Jesus was God with us.

3

The Lame Will Walk

Messiah's Miracles

If I could have one gift of God's power, it would be the power to heal. What a thrill it would be to touch a young boy's arm ravaged by cancer and to see that arm made whole! I've prayed for people to be healed and have seen some wonderful demonstrations of God's healing work, but I would like to be able to be the channel through which God would empty hospital wards and cancer clinics by his healing power.

GROUP DISCUSSION. What would you do if you were given the gift of God's healing power for one hour—and what would be the potential dangers of possessing healing ability?

PERSONAL REFLECTION. Where in your life do you need God's healing—in a relationship? In your body? From past failures? Open your heart to the Lord as you begin this study and ask him to begin the healing process.

The prophet Isaiah, more than any other Old Testament

prophet, was given a picture of what the world would look like when God's promised Redeemer would come. One of the prominent marks of God's presence in the Messiah would be the reversal of sin's curse in the lives of those he touched. *Read Isaiah 35:3-6.*

_____

1. Describe the spiritual and emotional condition of the people Isaiah is addressing (vv. 3-4).

What stress factors in your life right now are causing your hands and knees to tremble or your heart to fear?

_____

2. What kinds of events will happen to the land and the people God saves (vv. 5-6)?

_____

3. Which of these miraculous acts seems most difficult and why?

Read Matthew 11:1-6.

4. John the Baptist had been sent by God to announce to the people of Israel the soon arrival of God's kingdom. What about Jesus' ministry and John's personal situation would raise doubts in John's mind (vv. 1-2)?

_____

5. What kinds of experiences tend to make you doubt God's goodness or provision or promises?

_____

6. Do you think Jesus was disappointed by John's question? Explain.

_____

7. How does Jesus' reply compare with what Isaiah had foreseen about the Messiah?

What conclusion would Jesus want John to draw?

8. In what ways might Jesus demonstrate this aspect of his messiahship in your life?

---

9. What would you ask him to touch or heal or restore first?

Ask Jesus to infuse your life with his power and encouragement.

Now or Later

Part 1, scene 5 of Handel's *Messiah* tells some of the wonderful things that will happen as a result of the Messiah's birth. Israel will rejoice and find peace in Messiah's eventual reign as king. Isaiah 35:3-6 is spoken just as the Isaiah 7:14 passage—"the virgin will conceive"—was spoken (see study 2). The miracles of Isaiah 35 are followed by the aria, "He shall feed His flock," in which Jesus is portrayed as our comforting shepherd. The aria ends with an invitation, sung by the soprano: "Come unto Him, all ye that labour and are heavy laden, and He will give you rest."

Take the time to listen to the entire scene 5 of part 1. Think about Jesus' care for you and his gracious invitation to rest in him.

4

Why Have You Forsaken Me?

Messiah's Death

Tragedies have a way of imprinting themselves on our minds. Some of us can remember the day in 1963 when we heard that President John Kennedy had been assassinated. Most of us can recall the morning of September 11, 2001, when passenger planes flew into the towers of the World Trade Center. But imagine what it would be like to have a document written one thousand years earlier that pictured these events in detail—that a world leader, for example, would die from a piece of metal hurled at his head from a long distance as he traveled down the street of a large city in a carriage not drawn by horses. We would hold such a document in awe and wonder at the writer's source of knowledge. But such a document would not begin to compare to Psalm 22. David, under God's direction, gives us startling images of a crucifixion hundreds of years before anyone was put to death on a cross.

GROUP DISCUSSION. Have you ever predicted some aspect of a future event—the outcome of a ball game, the gender of an unborn child, the budding romance or marriage of a friend? Share your story with the group. What did you base your prediction on?

PERSONAL REFLECTION. What insights do you have about your personal future? What do you know for sure—and what do you hope will happen?

Psalm 22 is an amazing portrayal of the persecution and execution of a righteous person. I'm sure David felt and experienced some of these things as he faced the hatred and oppression of his enemies. But the Holy Spirit spoke about more than David's personal experience in this psalm. The Spirit moved David to write about another righteous man who would suffer a horrific death more than one thousand years later. *Read Psalm 22:1-21.*

---

1. As you scan through this section of Psalm 22 again, which verses are expressions of anguish and which are expressions of confidence in the Lord's presence and ability to help?

What does that movement between anguish and confidence tell you about the sufferer?

---

2. The psalm begins with a desperate cry addressed to "my God." Matthew and Mark in the New Testament record this same cry from Jesus on the cross (Matthew 27:46; Mark 15:34). When have you felt abandoned by God?

Does it help to know that Jesus felt the same way? Explain.

---

3. What does the righteous sufferer in the psalm draw upon for assurance and comfort (vv. 3-5)?

---

4. What past acts of God's faithfulness can you draw upon when you feel like God is far from you?

---

5. Which is worse: feeling abandoned by God or enduring the insults of other people (vv. 6-8)? Why?

---

6. Is this sufferer an evil person living under the consequences of his own rebellion? (Read his testimony in verses 9-11.) Why then has he been rejected?

---

7. From what you know of Jesus' crucifixion, point out details in verses 12-18 that picture the death Jesus would die.

---

8. How does the psalm describe the physical condition of the sufferer (vv. 14-17)?

What might you conclude about the guilt or innocence of an individual in this condition?

_____

9. What can you learn from verses 19-21 about the attitude of Jesus during his agony on the cross?

How does his example encourage you in your difficult days?

Express your pain or sorrow or discouragement honestly to the Lord. Follow that with expressions of confident trust in him. You might even pray verses 19-21 to the Lord.

Now or Later

The second section of scene 1, part 2 of Handel's *Messiah* takes us to the cross. We hear the abusive shouts of onlookers and the mockery of the crowd. Jesus looked for some to have pity on him but found none. The music and the text are designed to break our hearts. The tenor soloist sings "Behold" four times— "Behold, and see if there be any sorrow like unto His sorrow."

Listen to the last part of scene 1, part 2 in a quiet setting. Let the music sweep over you and let the words break up any hard places in your heart of indifference or rebellion or unresponsiveness to the Lord.

5

Pierced for Our Transgressions

Messiah's Sacrifice

We call it heroic when someone risks or gives their life to rescue or protect others—the soldier who puts himself in the path of enemy fire to rescue a wounded comrade, the fire fighter who runs into a burning home to make sure no one is left behind, a bystander who pulls an injured person to safety from a wrecked car. Sometimes the hero is the person we would least expect to act so bravely. Sometimes we are the ones who are placed in situations that call for courage and sacrifice.

GROUP DISCUSSION. What national or local person is a hero to you? Why?

PERSONAL REFLECTION. What person in your life has been a model of self-sacrifice, and how has that person influenced you?

As God began to reveal aspects of the coming Messiah's character and ministry to the Old Testament prophets, one mark of the Messiah became shockingly clear: he would suffer more deeply than any other human being. Most people didn't like that part of the Messiah's ministry. They liked the victorious conqueror side of God's Anointed One and the miracles of healing and power, but not so much the suffering side.

Isaiah saw the Messiah in his glory, but he also got a long, painful look at the Messiah's humiliation. In Isaiah 53 the servant of the Lord (Isaiah 52:13) is despised by his own people and struck down by his own Father. *Read Isaiah 53:1-10.*

---

1. If this passage was all we had in the Bible about God's promised Redeemer, what qualities would you look for in someone who claimed to be the Messiah?

Do you find those qualities in Jesus? Explain.

---

2. According to verse 2, how would you describe the Messiah's childhood if he grew up next door to you?

---

3. How did Isaiah picture the treatment of the Messiah by the people around him (vv. 3, 7-8)?

---

4. Those who looked on as the Messiah suffered would consider him stricken down by God in judgment for his own sins (v. 4), but what was the true purpose of his suffering and who was he suffering for (vv. 4-6)?

_____

5. Isaiah uses the language of sacrifice in verses 7 and 10. How does that make the Servant's death more than just a martyr's death for a good cause?

_____

6. The New Testament applies this passage at least seven times to Jesus. Using these verses in Isaiah, how would you explain Jesus' suffering and death to someone who wanted to know more about him?

_____

7. How does this understanding of Jesus' death bring assurance to you of God's love and forgiveness?

_____

8. What encouragement to sacrificial service does this Servant's example bring to you even if other people turn against you or misunderstand you?

_____

9. What hope for the Messiah do you find in verse 10? Is his rejection and death the whole story?

10. What confident hope does the Christian have who sacrifices him- or herself in obedience to God and in devoted service to others?

Spend a few minutes pondering Jesus' sacrifice for you. Re-read Isaiah 53 putting your name in the text as the recipient of Jesus' suffering. Give thanks to Jesus for his willing sacrifice in your place.

Now or Later

The text of Isaiah 53 is used extensively by Handel in the first part of scene 1, part 2 of *Messiah*. Scene 1 is by far the largest and longest scene in the oratorio. The first aria is the longest in the entire composition.

This section obviously proclaims the central theme of the story Handel wants to tell. The sacrifice of Jesus on the cross is of crucial importance, and we hear it over and over: "He was despised and rejected of men, a man of sorrows, and acquainted with grief." For more than ten minutes the focus is on *what* Jesus suffered; in the following three choruses the focus is on those *for whom* Jesus suffered—"Surely He hath borne *our* griefs . . . with His stripes *we* are healed . . . the Lord hath laid on Him the iniquity of *us* all."

It is worth the investment of time to listen to the entire first half of section 1, part 2. Enter into the mood of the music as you contemplate Jesus' suffering in your place and for your sins. Express your relief and gratitude that Jesus was willing to pay the full penalty that you deserved.

6

The Path of Life

Messiah's Resurrection

Psalm 16:7-11; Acts 2:22-32

I've had to do a lot of thinking about the future lately. As I look down the road of life, I see some big changes coming and I've been wrestling with the uncertainties of it all—how to take care of an aging mother, what the next step is in my career, whether we will have the financial resources to help our kids and grandkids. At the same time, I have a peace about the future that only comes from knowing the Lord. He has never failed to care for us in times of plenty and in times of struggle. We have promises that extend throughout life and even far beyond. Jesus will never forsake us, and even death cannot separate us from the love of Christ.

GROUP DISCUSSION. What are some of your concerns as you look at your future? What experiences in the past help to calm your heart about the future?

PERSONAL REFLECTION. When you think of death, do you change the subject? Tremble inside? Have a sense of confidence? Why do you feel the way you do?

David wrote Psalm 16 as he thought about the whole scope
of his life. God had blessed him in wonderful ways and surrounded him with godly people. David had faced his share of
enemies but God had always seen him through. Even when
David thought about his final enemy, death, he knew that God
would show him the path of life forever. What David may not
have realized as he wrote is that the words of his psalm had far
greater significance than just for David. He spoke as a prophet
about a greater king yet to come. *Read Psalm 16:7-11.*

---

1. As you read back through this short passage again, what was
David confident of from the Lord?

---

2. What did David do to have such a confident view of life and
the future (v. 8)?

---

3. Which of David's assertions are you most confident of for
your life?

Which are you not so confident about?

---

4. What specifically did David believe about his existence and
relationship with God beyond death (vv. 10-11)?

5. Did David's hope for the future come true? In what way?

In the New Testament the apostle Peter says that David's words had a greater fulfillment in the life of the promised Messiah. David's words were more than just a promise about his own future; he also spoke of David's greater son, Jesus. *Read Acts 2:22-32.*

---

6. As Peter preaches the message about Jesus to his own nation, what does Peter emphasize about

• Jesus' ministry (v. 22)?

• Jesus' death (v. 23)?

• the next event (v. 24)?

---

7. Since Peter's point to the people of Israel is that Jesus was the promised Messiah, he goes to the Scriptures to validate his claim that Jesus was raised from the dead. King David died and his body was still in the ground. What is Peter trying to get his audience to realize about Psalm 16?

---

8. When you talk to another person about who Jesus is, do you focus more on his death in our place or on his resurrection from the dead? Which is more important?

---

9. The promise of the Messiah's resurrection was embedded in the sacred writings of the Old Testament. The fulfillment of that promise was confirmed by the eyewitness testimony of the apostles. Why do *you* believe that Jesus rose from the dead?

Pray that the reality of Jesus' resurrection will give you great confidence in God's presence in your personal future—in this life and beyond this life.

Now or Later

The moment of Jesus' death is simply announced in *Messiah*, part 2, scene 2—"He was cut off out of the land of the living" (Isaiah 53:8). But death was not the end for Jesus. There is no musical account in *Messiah* of Jesus' burial or the earthquake or the women at the tomb. Instead the resurrection is proclaimed in the words of Psalm 16:10—"But Thou didst not leave His soul in hell." The minor keys of scene 1 give way to major keys in scene 2. Jens Larsen writes: "From the beginning of the aria we are in a new world, above all earthly torment and death, freed from darkness and the oppression of hell" (Jens Peter Larsen, *Handel's Messiah: Origins, Composition, Sources* [New York: W. W. Norton, 1957], p. 150).

As you listen to scene 2, enter into the joy of Jesus' resurrection. Because death was not the end for him, neither will it be for us.

7

Lift Up Your Heads
Messiah's Exaltation

Psalm 24

The British people know what royalty is all about! Americans are citizens of a republic; Brits are subjects of the current king or queen. It might surprise most of us who don't live under the rule of a king or queen to know that God's ideal government is an absolute monarchy—but with the right person on the throne!

Jesus rules as King over all the universe. During his earthly ministry, Jesus' glory and majesty were hidden. He lived among us as a human being—no glow, no halo. Even after his resurrection, Jesus still looked like one of us. But at his ascension into heaven and to the right hand of the Father, Jesus took upon himself all the glory he had before he came to earth. He stands in heaven as a resurrected human being, but he shines brighter in majesty than the sun.

GROUP DISCUSSION. What royal person would you like to meet? What would you say to him or her?

PERSONAL REFLECTION. When you think of Jesus, how do you picture him? What elements of majesty enter your mind?

Psalms 22–24 form a triptych—a threefold portrait of the Messiah. In Psalm 22 we have a picture of Jesus in the past—the suffering Savior dying a humiliating death. In Psalm 23 we see Jesus in the present—the caring Shepherd guarding and guiding his sheep. Then in Psalm 24 we have a song about Jesus in the future—the conquering King returning and reigning in splendor. *Read Psalm 24.*

---

1. What does David emphasize about God in the first two verses, and why is that truth important for a proper view of God's majesty?

---

2. What does it mean to "ascend the mountain of the LORD" or to "stand in his holy place" (v. 3)?

How do we do those things today?

---

3. Explain in present-day terms what David says is required of those who would stand accepted before the Lord (v. 4).

What can those who seek the Lord in this way expect to receive (vv. 5-6)?

4. The imagery of verses 7-10 is of a victorious king returning to Jerusalem in triumph. What aspects of this great king's character does David emphasize?

---

5. How does this entrance of a mighty king contrast with Jesus' first coming to earth?

---

6. In what ways can we acknowledge and celebrate the majesty and authority of Jesus in our lives?

---

7. How can we display Jesus' glory and majesty in our corporate worship?

Do you leave the worship service at your church with the realization that you have been in the presence of the King of glory? Why or why not?

Express your allegiance and loyalty to Jesus as King. Humble yourself before him with your words and actions.

Now or Later

As we've seen in this study, verses 7-10 of Psalm 24 depict the return of a victorious king from battle. The Messiah, the King of glory, returns to the splendor of heaven in victory over sin, Satan and death.

The chorus Handel composed to celebrate Jesus' ascension is unique among the choruses of *Messiah*; it is the work's only antiphonal chorus. The higher voices of the choir announce the King's coming; the lower voices respond with the question, "Who is the King of glory?" Back and forth the voices ring in a stirring anthem of praise.

Listen to (or sing) part 2, scene 3 ("Lift up your heads, O ye gates") with joy-filled enthusiasm. Picture Jesus returning to heaven and reclaiming his place of majesty and authority at God's right hand.

8

The Clouds of Heaven

Messiah's Return

Daniel 7:9-14; Revelation 19:1-16

You can still watch the video on YouTube. It takes place in a mall food court. People are eating and talking in the hustle of Christmas shopping when a woman who seems to be an ordinary shopper stands up and sings the opening lines of the "Hallelujah Chorus" from Handel's *Messiah*. The woman is soon joined by other singers. The whole act has been choreographed to surprise and bless the shoppers. In a few moments all the shoppers in the food court are on their feet, carrying on the tradition of standing during this magnificent chorus of praise to Jesus, the conquering King.

The tradition began when *Messiah* was first performed in London in 1743. King George II was in the audience. No one knows exactly why he stood up when the first notes of the "Hallelujah Chorus" were played, but when the king stood, everyone else stood. It has been the tradition to stand during this wonderful piece ever since. Almost one hundred years later, Queen Victoria was at a performance of *Messiah*, sitting in a wheelchair. As the "Hallelujah Chorus" began, she struggled to her feet. Later she remarked, "I will not sit in the presence of the King of kings."

GROUP DISCUSSION. Tell the group about a time when the words or majesty of a song caused you to respond in some outward way—stand, kneel, applaud, weep, raise your hands. Who were you responding to?

PERSONAL REFLECTION. What is your normal posture in worship? In prayer? What might a new posture express to the Lord?

The writers of the Old Testament not only caught a glimpse of a suffering Messiah and a victorious Messiah, they also saw a coming Messiah. God's promised Redeemer would burst out of heaven and reclaim all that Adam had lost. The Messiah would take back his world, rescue his people and destroy his enemies. The prophet Daniel watched a series of evil wild beasts stalk the earth, ravishing God's people and crushing all who stood against them. Suddenly Daniel's eyes were drawn to heaven and a very different scene unfolded there. God was about to reclaim what was rightly his. *Read Daniel 7:9-14.*

---

1. Daniel sees a powerful figure seated on heaven's throne, "the Ancient of Days." What does each element of Daniel's description convey to you about the character and ability of this heavenly being?

Clothing:

Hair:

Throne:

River:

Attendants:

Who do you conclude the Ancient of Days is?

---

2. The earthly "beast" and the evil "horn" (see v. 8) are destroyed by God's power (vv. 11-12). These images represent worldly power and evil rulers. What does their destruction tell you about the future of all human government?

---

3. The Ancient of Days hands dominion and power to another being—"one like a son of man." This person is obviously human. What aspects of Daniel's description in verses 13-14 lead you to believe that he is more than a human being?

---

4. How do you respond to the evil, "beastly" forces and events in our world?

What heavenly perspective does this passage give you on the present and the future?

The prophecy of Daniel 7 is picked up by the author of the book of Revelation as he describes the future return of Jesus to the earth in majesty and power. *Read Revelation 19:1-16.*

---

5. Compare the five songs or shouts of praise in this passage (vv. 1-2, 3, 4, 5, 6-8). What is the emphasis of each one?

What do you learn about the character of God in these refrains?

---

6. Where do you see yourself in these verses—falling down in worship (v. 4), invited to the wedding supper (v. 9), riding out of heaven (v. 14), being struck down under God's wrath (v. 15)? Explain.

---

7. How does Jesus' ultimate triumph over evil and injustice affect your view of life's struggles here and now?

---

8. What names are given to Jesus in verses 11-16 and what does each name reveal to you about Jesus' character and power?

Which name gives you the most confidence as you face tomorrow? Explain.

Compose a song or shout of praise to Jesus for his goodness, grace and power in your life. Sing or read it to the group—and to the Lord as an act of worship.

Now or Later

In Handel's *Messiah* the famous "Hallelujah Chorus" immediately follows the account of Christ's victory over his enemies. Some have called this section a "coronation anthem" in which Jesus is revealed as the King over all kings. In three and a half minutes Handel packs all the jubilation and pomp necessary for such an occasion. The passage reaches a stirring climax with the phrases "King of Kings" and "He shall reign" echoing over and over. Then comes a flurry of eight "forevers" and "hallelujahs," a grand pause, and the final powerful "Hal-le-lu-jah!"

If your group can sing (or wants to try), pass out the score of the "Hallelujah Chorus" and let everyone sing along with the recorded version (standing, of course). You might also put together a small orchestra and choir, and sing the piece as part of your worship service at your church. It's traditionally sung at Christmas or Easter but can be sung any time as an expression of praise and adoration to Jesus.

Leader's Notes

Leading a Bible discussion can be an enjoyable and rewarding experience. But it can also be *scary*—especially if you've never done it before. If this is your feeling, you're in good company. When God asked Moses to lead the Israelites out of Egypt, he replied, "O Lord, please send someone else to do it!" (Ex 4:13). It was the same with Solomon, Jeremiah and Timothy, but God helped these people in spite of their weaknesses, and he will help you as well.

You don't need to be an expert on the Bible or a trained teacher to lead a Bible discussion. The idea behind these inductive studies is that the leader guides group members to discover for themselves what the Bible has to say. This method of learning will allow group members to remember much more of what is said than a lecture would.

These studies are designed to be led easily. As a matter of fact, the flow of questions through the passage from observation to interpretation to application is so natural that you may feel that the studies lead themselves. This study guide is also flexible. You can use it with a variety of groups—student, professional, neighborhood or church groups. Each study takes forty-five to sixty minutes in a group setting.

There are some important facts to know about group dynamics and encouraging discussion. The suggestions listed below should enable you to effectively and enjoyably fulfill your role as leader.

Preparing for the Study

1. Ask God to help you understand and apply the passage in your own life. Unless this happens, you will not be prepared to lead others. Pray too for the various members of the group. Ask God to open your hearts to the message of his Word and motivate you to action.

2. Read the introduction to the entire guide to get an overview of the entire book and the issues which will be explored.

3. As you begin each study, read and reread the assigned Bible passage to familiarize yourself with it.

4. This study guide is based on the New International Version of the Bible. It will help you and the group if you use this translation as the basis for your study and discussion.

5. Carefully work through each question in the study. Spend time in meditation and reflection as you consider how to respond.

6. Write your thoughts and responses in the space provided in the study guide. This will help you to express your understanding of the passage clearly.

7. It might help to have a Bible dictionary handy. Use it to look up any unfamiliar words, names or places. (For additional help on how to study a passage, see chapter five of *How to Lead a LifeGuide Bible Study*, InterVarsity Press.)

8. Consider how you can apply the Scripture to your life. Remember that the group will follow your lead in responding to the studies. They will not go any deeper than you do.

9. Once you have finished your own study of the passage, familiarize yourself with the leader's notes for the study you are leading. These are designed to help you in several ways. First, they tell you the purpose the study guide author had in mind when writing the study. Take time to think through how the study questions work together to accomplish that purpose. Second, the notes provide you with additional background information or suggestions on group dynamics for various questions. This information can be useful when people have difficulty understanding or answering a question. Third, the leader's notes can alert you to potential problems you may encounter during the study.

10. If you wish to remind yourself of anything mentioned in the leader's notes, make a note to yourself below that question in the study.

Leading the Study

1. Begin the study on time. Open with prayer, asking God to help the group to understand and apply the passage.

2. Be sure that everyone in your group has a study guide. Encourage the group to prepare beforehand for each discussion by reading the introduction to the guide and by working through the questions in the study.

3. At the beginning of your first time together, explain that these studies are meant to be discussions, not lectures. Encourage the members of the group to participate. However, do not put pressure on those who may be hesitant to speak during the first few sessions. You may want to suggest the following guidelines to your group.

☐ Stick to the topic being discussed.

☐ Your responses should be based on the verses which are the focus of the discussion and not on outside authorities such as commentaries or speakers.

☐ These studies focus on a particular passage of Scripture. Only rarely should you refer to other portions of the Bible. This allows for everyone to participate in in-depth study on equal ground.

☐ Anything said in the group is considered confidential and will not be discussed outside the group unless specific permission is given to do so.

☐ We will listen attentively to each other and provide time for each person present to talk.

☐ We will pray for each other.

4. Have a group member read the introduction at the beginning of the discussion.

5. Every session begins with a group discussion question. The question or activity is meant to be used before the passage is read. The question introduces the theme of the study and encourages group members to begin to open up. Encourage as many members as possible to participate, and be ready to get the discussion going with your own response.

This section is designed to reveal where our thoughts or feelings need to be transformed by Scripture. That is why it is especially important not to read the passage before the discussion question is asked. The passage will tend to color the honest reactions people would otherwise give because they are, of course, supposed to think the way the Bible does.

You may want to supplement the group discussion question with an icebreaker to help people to get comfortable. See the community section of *Small Group Idea Book* for more ideas.

You also might want to use the personal reflection question with your group. Either allow a time of silence for people to respond individually or discuss it together.

6. Have a group member (or members if the passage is long) read aloud the passage to be studied. Then give people several minutes to read the passage again silently so that they can take it all in.

7. Question 1 will generally be an overview question designed to briefly survey the passage. Encourage the group to look at the whole passage, but try to avoid getting sidetracked by questions or issues that will be addressed later in the study.

8. As you ask the questions, keep in mind that they are designed to be used just as they are written. You may simply read them aloud. Or you may prefer to express them in your own words.

There may be times when it is appropriate to deviate from the study guide. For example, a question may have already been answered. If so, move on to the next question. Or someone may raise an important question not covered in the guide. Take time to discuss it, but try to keep the group from going off on tangents.

9. Avoid answering your own questions. If necessary, repeat or rephrase them until they are clearly understood. Or point out something you read in the leader's notes to clarify the context or meaning. An eager group quickly becomes passive and silent if they think the leader will do most of the talking.

10. Don't be afraid of silence. People may need time to think about the question before formulating their answers.

11. Don't be content with just one answer. Ask, "What do the rest of you think?" or "Anything else?" until several people have given answers to the question.

12. Acknowledge all contributions. Try to be affirming whenever possible. Never reject an answer. If it is clearly off-base, ask, "Which verse led you to that conclusion?" or again, "What do the rest of you think?"

13. Don't expect every answer to be addressed to you, even though this will probably happen at first. As group members become more at ease, they will begin to truly interact with each other. This is one sign of healthy discussion.

14. Don't be afraid of controversy. It can be very stimulating. If you don't resolve an issue completely, don't be frustrated. Move on and keep it in mind for later. A subsequent study may solve the problem.

15. Periodically summarize what the group has said about the passage. This helps to draw together the various ideas mentioned and gives continuity to the study. But don't preach.

16. At the end of the Bible discussion you may want to allow group members a time of quiet to work on an idea under "Now or Later." Then discuss what you experienced. Or you may want to encourage group members to work on these ideas between meetings. Give an opportunity during the session for people to talk about what they are learning.

17. Conclude your time together with conversational prayer, adapting the prayer suggestion at the end of the study to your group. Ask for God's help in following through on the commitments you've made.

18. End on time.

Many more suggestions and helps are found in *How to Lead a LifeGuide Bible Study.*

Components of Small Groups

A healthy small group should do more than study the Bible. There are four components to consider as you structure your time together.

Nurture. Small groups help us to grow in our knowledge and love of God. Bible study is the key to making this happen and is the foundation of your small group.

Community. Small groups are a great place to develop deep friendships with other Christians. Allow time for informal interaction before and after each study. Plan activities and games that will help you get to know each other. Spend time having fun together going on a picnic or cooking dinner together.

Worship and prayer. Your study will be enhanced by spending time praising God together in prayer or song. Pray for each other's needs and keep track of how God is answering prayer in your group. Ask God to help you to apply what you are learning in your study.

Outreach. Reaching out to others can be a practical way of applying what you are learning, and it will keep your group from becoming self-focused. Host a series of evangelistic discussions for your friends or neighbors. Clean up the yard of an elderly friend. Serve at a soup kitchen together, or spend a day working on a Habitat house.

Many more suggestions and helps in each of these areas are found in *Small Group Idea Book.* Information on building a small group can be found in *Small Group Leaders' Handbook* and *The Big Book on Small Groups* (both from InterVarsity Press). Reading through one of these books would be worth your time.

Study 1. His Name Is Wonderful. Isaiah 9:6-7.

Purpose: To introduce Jesus as the Messiah and to explore his incredible character.

Question 1. The person Isaiah talks about is called a "child" and a "son." He is a human child who is "born." This child will also reign on David's throne over an earthly kingdom. But Isaiah uses other phrases to describe this person that make him more than human. He will reign but his kingdom will have "no end," and he will rule "forever." How can a mere human child also be called "Mighty God"?

Questions 2-3. The first title given to this promised one is "Wonderful Counselor." The first person we call or turn to in a crisis is the person we trust the most. Where the Lord fits on that list of those we go to in a time of need tells us how much we have learned to rely on Jesus as our Counselor and Guide. Jesus usually guides us through his Word, but he may also direct us by the Spirit, by circumstances or by insights that come from faith.

Question 5. When we are linked by faith to Jesus, we enjoy eternal blessings immediately. The believer has eternal life—a whole new kind of life lived in a new realm. We are indwelt by God's eternal Spirit and learn what it means to be directed by him. The Christian is "in Christ" and Christ is "in us," so we have access to a person who is the source of wisdom and right decisions.

Question 7. This is the first of several questions in this study guide in which the participant is asked to reflect on his or her personal belief or relationship with the Lord and to reveal possible areas of struggle or doubt. You, the leader, need to give each person the freedom and safety to answer without fear of judgment or condemnation from you or any other group member. When difficult issues are expressed, approach them with compassion and understanding. The goal is to help each person work through these areas of struggle with the Lord's help.

Question 8. Isaiah saw the glory of the Messiah's kingdom more clearly than any other Old Testament prophet. God's Anointed One will reign forever in sovereign authority over all creation. He will not reign as a cruel tyrant but with unerring justice and absolute righteousness. The Messiah will always do what is right and good. Human beings will flourish under his rule.

Question 9. Some Christians have the idea that submitting to Jesus' lordship will be constricting and oppressive, but Jesus promised an easy yoke and rest for those who are weary. The life committed fully to Jesus is a life of purpose and joy and fulfillment. The empty endeavors and frustrations of a life lived only for pleasure or gain or fame are replaced with peace and confidence that our lives are bringing glory to God. Submitting to Jesus is not so much "giving in" to his demands as it is "giving over" in willing obedience to his gracious and loving reign as King and Lord.

Study 2. The Virgin Will Be with Child. Isaiah 7:1-16; Matthew 1:18-25.

Purpose: To grasp the significance of God the Son coming as a human being to be God with us.

Question 1. In 734 BC the nation of Judah came under enormous pressure from surrounding nations to join a coalition that would try to stop the westward expansion of the Assyrian Empire. Ahaz, king of Judah, refused to join and, as a result, found himself under attack. King Rezin of Syria and King Pekah of Israel (or Ephraim) invaded Judah with the goal of either forcing Ahaz to join their coalition or replacing Ahaz with a puppet king.

Question 3. The Lord told Ahaz that the coalition would fail in their objective. Furthermore, within a few years Aram (Syria) would be conquered (Isaiah implies in verse 8 that Rezin will be Aram's final king) and within sixty-five years Israel would be shattered and the people scattered. Actually, within twelve years of Isaiah's prophecy (722 BC), Assyria conquered the northern kingdom on Israel and over time the people were forced to move to other parts of the empire. Certainly within the sixty-five years of the prophecy (v. 8), the nation that now threatened Judah would be just a memory. Ahaz's responsibility was to believe what God had said and to remain faithful to the Lord. If Ahaz sought help from any other source, his kingdom would fall.

Question 4. Isaiah uses the Hebrew word *'almah* to refer to a young and probably unmarried woman at the time. By the time this woman conceives a child and gives birth, and the child can discern between what is harmful to him and what is not harmful, about three years would elapse. By then the two invading kings would be gone from Judean soil. In Matthew's translation of Isaiah 7:14 in Matthew 1:23, he uses the Greek word *parthenos* which specifically means a virgin woman.

Stan Guthrie adds, "Jews in Joseph's (Mary's promised husband) time probably saw Isaiah 7:14 as both fulfilled in the prophet's life and also as a larger messianic prediction. . . . Therefore, Jews such as Joseph viewed this prediction as having a larger, miraculous fulfillment—Immanuel, *God*, would be with them" (Stan Guthrie, *A Concise Guide to Bible Prophecy* [Grand Rapids: Baker, 2013], p. 91).

Question 5. Both the sign and the fulfillment required Ahaz to wait. All he had to rely on was the word of the Lord through Isaiah the prophet. God used this experience as a test for Ahaz and the people of Judah—would they trust God even if it took a while, or would they seek immediate help from another direction and forfeit God's blessing? We face the same struggle when we trust God to work in a problem situation or relationship rather than plunging in on our own.

Question 6. Joseph loved Mary and didn't want to see her publicly humiliated. At the same time, Joseph was a righteous man. He knew that he was not the father of Mary's child, and so he could only come to one conclusion—that Mary had been unfaithful to him. Joseph's relationship to the Lord is revealed in his willingness to believe the angel's message and his immediate obedience to what the angel told him to do.

Question 7. Matthew verifies the reality of Mary's miraculous pregnancy by appealing to Scripture. What Matthew finds in Isaiah's prophecy is affirmation that the Messiah would be born of a virgin. This prophecy would have brought peace to Joseph's troubled heart. Not only did he have the angel's message but he also had the more certain words of Scripture on which to act.

Question 8. Isaiah said the child would be regarded as Immanuel, which Matthew correctly translates as "God with us." In the historical fulfillment of this prophecy in Isaiah's own day, the child who was born (perhaps to Ahaz's wife or even to Isaiah's wife) was a sign that God was with his people, protecting and helping them. When Jesus was born as the prophetic fulfillment of Isaiah's prophecy, the child would be more than human—fully human but also fully God.

Question 9. Because Jesus is God, he can minister to and care for all his people at once. Whatever trial we face, Jesus stands with us—and all the power of God is at his disposal.

Study 3. The Lame Will Walk. Isaiah 35:3-6; Matthew 11:1-6.
Purpose: To focus on Jesus' willingness to work powerfully in our lives and through us in the lives of others.

Question 1. Isaiah gave these promises to people who were under the threat of conquest by the cruel Assyrian army (see Is 36). The people of Judah were filled with fear and felt like God had abandoned his people. In spite of the external dangers, Isaiah calls them to trust God and to believe his promise of a future, powerful intervention by the Lord on behalf of those who have faith in him.

Give the members of the group the freedom and safety to talk honestly about their struggles and fears.

Question 2. God's visitation to his people ("your God will come" [v. 4]) will produce astonishing results. The effects of sin's curse on human beings will be reversed. Even the natural world will respond to God's presence by bursting into new life.

Question 3. Isaiah chooses some of the most difficult of miracles as the marks of God's arrival among his people—the blind will see, the deaf will hear. Of course, to an all-powerful God, no miracle is more difficult than another, but these miracles will be a source of wonder and joy to those who receive them.

Question 4. John the Baptist had been certain that Jesus of Nazareth was the promised Messiah. But Jesus wasn't acting as John expected the Messiah to act. It didn't seem to John that the long-anticipated kingdom of God was being ushered in as he had expected and proclaimed it would be. Furthermore, John languished in prison. He was put there by Herod Antipas for preaching against Herod's marriage to his brother's wife (see Mt 14:1-5). These factors raised doubts in John's mind about Jesus—was he really the Anointed One or not?

Question 6. Jesus certainly understood John's struggle, and he tries through his response to reassure John that he was indeed the Messiah. Some students of Matthew's Gospel see a mild rebuke to John in Jesus' final words to the messengers (v. 6). When Jesus spoke once again to the crowd, however, he made this declaration about John: "Among those born of women there has not risen anyone greater than John" (Mt 11:11).

Question 7. Jesus wanted John to link the events of Jesus' ministry to the prophecies in Isaiah about the Messiah's miracles. "Jesus does not answer the question directly but simply points to the messianic words and deeds that are proof of his messianic office" (Grant Osborne, *Matthew*, Zondervan Exegetical Commentary on the New Testament [Grand Rapids: Zondervan, 2010], p. 415). The messianic age had now arrived in Jesus!

In Matthew 8–9 the author records exactly the miracles Jesus talks about in his response to John—healing the blind (9:27-31), healing the lame (9:1-8), cleansing a leper (8:1-4), healing the deaf (9:32-34) and raising the dead (9:18-24). The preaching of good news to the poor is recorded in Matthew 9:35-36. These continuing fulfillments of Isaiah's prophecy are what the messengers were to report back to John the Baptist.

Questions 8-9. Jesus may choose to work in our lives in miraculous power or he may choose not to. The point is that Jesus' new life and power are available to us. Even if we feel imprisoned by current circumstances, we are called to trust him fully and to look with eager anticipation for his intervention in our lives.

Study 4. Why Have You Forsaken Me? Psalm 22:1-21.
Purpose: To see Jesus as our model for facing suffering with confident trust in God.
Introduction. Psalm 22 is the first passional psalm—a song that reflects extreme suffering. Psalms 35, 41, 55, 69, and 109 are also passional psalms. Psalm 22 is quoted more often in the New Testament than any other psalm, but the author is never identified in the New Testament quotations. David's authorship is confirmed by the heading of the psalm.

Walter Kaiser summarizes the view of most evangelical interpreters of Psalm 22: "David did experience unusual suffering, but under a revelation from God he witnesses the suffering of one of his offspring, presumably the last in that promised line, that far transcends anything that came his way" (Walter Kaiser, *The Messiah in the Old Testament* [Grand Rapids: Zondervan, 1995], p. 113).
Question 1. The sufferer feels abandoned by God, but that feeling does not mesh with what the writer knows about the character and past actions of the Lord. The writer knows God has been faithful to respond to his people and to rescue them from trouble (vv. 4-5), but at the same time he feels like God is ignoring him now (v. 2). God is his strength (v. 19), but the writer is close to death (v. 15).
Question 2. David's question in verse 1 (and Jesus' echo of the same question as he hung on the cross) is not a question of surprise or doubt. It's an exclamation, a rhetorical question. He is not seeking an answer as much as he is standing in shocked awe that such an event would ever happen. What circumstance in God's plan would bring him to abandon someone who had been faithful to him?

Questions 3-4. As the sufferer thinks back over the biblical story, he can recall example after example in which God intervened to rescue those who were in danger or in pain. These spiritual ancestors cried out to the Lord and the Lord responded quickly and powerfully. God's faithful acts in the past brought encouragement as the sufferer patiently waited for God's deliverance.

Question 6. There had to be some other explanation for the righteous person's suffering. It simply could not be secret sin or moral corruption. If he was not standing under God's judgment for his own sin, there had to be another purpose for the suffering he was enduring. In Jesus' case, he was suffering God's judgment in the place of others. Those looking on were drawing an easy conclusion about the sufferer, but it was the wrong conclusion.

Question 7. Even those with only a basic knowledge of Jesus' crucifixion should be able to point out a few details: crowds of soldiers and enemies surrounded the cross (vv. 12-13; see Mt 27:36-44; Lk 23:35-39); crucifixion was a torturous death (v. 14); Jesus suffered intense thirst (v. 15; see Jn 19:28); Jesus' hands and feet were pierced (v. 16; see Jn 20:27); Jesus hung virtually naked on the cross (v. 17); soldiers gambled for Jesus' clothes (v. 18; see Mt 27:35; Jn 19:23-24).

Question 8. The conclusion most onlookers came to as they witnessed Jesus' crucifixion was that he was dying under the curse and penalty of God for his blasphemy. Even today some people (including some Christians) look at a person in physical decline or illness and wonder what that person has done to deserve such treatment from God. Other Christians conclude (correctly, I think) that a suffering person is sharing in experiences common to all of us and that God may use physical illness to strengthen our faith and trust in him.

Question 9. In spite of the crushing pain of the cross, Jesus maintained his trust and confidence in his Father. He knew that when the sin-bearing was finished, the Father would come quickly to rescue him. Jesus set the example for us of patient endurance in suffering, linked to confident trust in the care and love of God for his people.

Study 5. Pierced for Our Transgressions. Isaiah 53:1-10.
Purpose: To help us realize that it was through the loss of all dignity, acclaim and even life that the Messiah accomplished his greatest work.
Introduction. This passage is part of the fourth and longest Servant song in Isaiah (42:1-4; 49:1-6; 50:4-9; 52:13–53:12). The "Servant" in each of the songs is the Messiah, "Israel" in its fullest expression (49:3).
Question 1. The person Isaiah portrays has his beginning in an obscure, unexpected place. He appears in a dry place—much like the out-of-the-way town of Nazareth where Jesus grew up. This person would not come to the world with wealth or power or influence, but as a common man, a laborer perhaps—or a carpenter. The Servant would know human suffering and would experience the depths of pain and rejection. Those looking on his cruel death would consider him to be under the righteous judgment of God. In reality, however, he would bear the weight of sin for others and bring healing by his pain. Jesus bore the physical pain of crucifixion to demonstrate the spiritual agony of being made sin. In his willing sacrifice for others, the Servant would be cut off from the land of the living.
Question 3. The Servant Messiah would be rejected and despised by the people around him. The Hebrew word translated "despised" in verse 3 "means to consider something or someone to be worthless, unworthy of attention. The Servant will not suffer a conscious and deliberate rejection so much as a hasty dismissal" (John Oswalt, *The Book of Isaiah, Chapters 40-66*, New International Commentary on the Old Testament [Grand Rapids: Eerdmans, 1998], p. 383). Jesus certainly had times of great popularity and acclaim, but when he began to reveal the spiritual demands of genuine discipleship, most people turned away. At his execution

the leaders of Israel looked on his death as the evidence of God's curse on Jesus. When Jesus had the opportunity speak in his own defense, he usually stood in silence. In the minds of most people then and now, this suffering Messiah can hardly be the one who will deliver us from the bondage of sin and death.

Question 4. "The sufferings of the Servant were not his own fault, as 'we' thought, but were in fact the result of 'our' sins, and resulted in 'our' healing" (Oswalt, p. 384). Jesus was carrying "the iniquity of us all" in his body on the cross.

Question 5. The imagery of sacrifice and the substitution of the righteous for the guilty pervades Isaiah's thoughts. Jesus did not simply die for a noble cause or as the result of misplaced justice. Jesus died in our place, in our stead, and because of his sacrifice the penalty of our sin has been fully paid forever. He died for sinners, not as a martyr for a cause.

Question 6. The writers of the New Testament interpreted the historical event of Jesus' execution through the lens of Old Testament sacrifice and through the insight given by the Holy Spirit. Jesus' death was the ultimate sacrifice for sin. He was made sin for us and was given the treatment we deserved before God. His suffering, pain and death bring spiritual healing to us who deserve God's wrath, not his grace.

Question 7. Jesus' death for sinners was the supreme expression of God's love for lost human beings. We deserved separation from God, but God himself made a way for the penalty of sin to be paid and, at the same time, to rescue believing sinners.

Question 8. The Servant persisted in doing the will of his Father even when it brought rejection, dismissal and death. We as followers of Jesus are called to follow him with the same willingness to sacrifice our lives for others. We need to remember too that just as Jesus was exalted because of his faithful endurance in suffering (Phil 2:8-9), we will also receive God's reward for patient endurance (Jas 1:12).

Question 9. Verse 10 gives us the first glimmer of hope that death is not the end for the Servant. He can take comfort in the fact that he has submitted fully to the Father, but there is also the promise of life beyond death when the Servant will see the wonder of what his death made possible. The idea of a renewal to life is expanded further in verses 11-12.

Question 10. Christians who give themselves to respond obediently to Jesus' call to take up their cross and follow him will have the assurance of receiving Jesus' reward in this life and in the age to come. The phrases the Bible typically applies to those favored by God are applied to the Servant and, by implication, to those who follow in his path—they will see their descendants (spiritual sons and daughters), they will live long lives (forever lives) and they will accomplish God's purposes for their lives.

Study 6. The Path of Life. Psalm 16:7-11; Acts 2:22-32.

Purpose: To be assured again of the reality of Jesus resurrection and of the validation of Jesus' ministry by God's act of power in raising Jesus from the dead.

Questions 1-2. David was confident of the Lord's guidance and advice. The Lord was at David's "right hand," the place of support and protection, and as a result David would not be shaken in his faith (v. 8). David was also confident that he would be with the Lord after death—at the Lord's right hand for eternity. David based that confidence on God's grace, which is received through faith in God's character and promises. "I keep my eyes always on the LORD" (v. 8) is an expression of ongoing faith and trust in the Lord.

Question 3. Allow group members to express what they are "not so confident" about honestly. The goal is not to instantly address their concerns as much as it is to lead them into a growing life of faith in the Lord.

Question 4. David believed that God would somehow preserve or keep his body, perhaps in anticipation of a future resurrection of the body. He was also confident that death would not separate him from the Lord's presence or the Lord's care. David knew that he would enjoy conscious fellowship with the Lord even after death.

Question 5. David eventually experienced physical death. His body was buried, and even though decay naturally set in, his body was not lost to God. In the future the seed of David's body that was planted in burial will be raised up as a glorious body designed to live forever. David's spirit was not abandoned by God but enjoys fellowship with God even today.

Question 6. The apostle Peter for the first time proclaims the message of the gospel, the good news of Jesus' life, death and resurrection, and its significance for the human race. Peter reviews facts that most of his hearers already knew, but he adds new significance by linking Jesus' ministry and death to his resurrection. Jesus' ministry marked him out as being sent and authorized by God as the Messiah. Jesus' death was no accident or tragic miscalculation; it fit into God's deliberate plan. Then came God's surprise—he raised Jesus from the dead!

Question 7. Jesus' resurrection should not have surprised anyone! Embedded in the Old Testament Scriptures was a prophecy that now can be fully understood. The prophecy in Psalm 16 never made complete sense if it was only about David, because David died and his body *did* see decay. His body was not forgotten by God, but it did return to the dust. Jesus' body, however, did not decay. The same body that was buried was raised to life. Jesus rose—body and spirit—from the dead. His resurrection was another validation that he was the Messiah, because the Scripture revealed that David's greater son would not be abandoned in the grave. He would be raised up again. Another use of Psalm 16:10 in the proclamation of the gospel is found in Acts 13:35-37.

Question 8. Neither aspect is "more important" than the other. Jesus' death and Jesus' resurrection are always linked in the message of the gospel.

Question 9. We believe in Jesus' resurrection based on the same two elements. The promised Messiah would not experience the decay of his body like David did, but would be raised from the dead before decay set in. We no longer hear the testimony of the eyewitnesses to the resurrection as the early Christians did, but we can read their testimony in written form preserved for us in the Bible. We also have the inner witness of the Holy Spirit who confirms the truth of the gospel to us, but that inner witness rests on the objective testimony of God's Word.

Study 7. Lift Up Your Heads. Psalm 24.

Purpose: To reaffirm our submission to Jesus as our mighty Lord and King.

Question 1. God's creation of the world, his ultimate ownership of all that is in it and his sovereign authority over all who live in it give us the context for appreciating God's majesty. The Lord is not some minor deity or a god with limitations. The Lord reigns over all. No being is greater or higher than he is.

Questions 2-3. David wrote in the context of the ark of the covenant, the place of God's visible presence with his people. Therefore, to come into God's immediate presence required worshipers to literally ascend to the city of Jerusalem and to present themselves in the place designated by God for worship. In this age, however, we can come confidently into God's presence anywhere. This passage is not just about coming to church. It is about making conscious preparation whenever or wherever we approach God in worship. Our hearts and lives are examined and our sins are confessed and our spirits are open to offer adoration to the Lord and to receive the blessings he desires to give. Our trust is in the Lord alone.

Question 4. Having gathered in the place of worship, the worshipers anticipate the arrival of the Lord himself. The command to "lift up your head" is symbolic of looking up in anticipation and hope. The gates of the city "look up" in preparation for the arrival of the great king. David emphasizes the power and greatness of the one who will arrive. We know this great king as Jesus Christ, who has been exalted to the highest place and given a name that is above every other name (Phil 2:9).

Question 5. Jesus' first coming to earth was quiet and humble, hardly the entrance of a great king. He was largely ignored and dismissed by his own people. He made his entrance into Jerusalem on a donkey, surrounded by peasant followers. Jesus' second coming to earth, on the other hand, will be far different. He will arrive as the King over all kings (Rev 19:11-16).

Question 6. Jesus already reigns in heaven and over his church as God's King. He also reigns as Lord in the hearts and lives of believers. We may not always live as if Jesus is Lord, but he is. As we submit ourselves to his authority and live as his loyal subjects, we display Jesus' glory to the people around us.

Question 7. We regularly acknowledge Jesus' friendship and love and grace in our worship. I wonder sometimes if we see or sing or acknowledge much of his majesty or authority over us as Lord and King. The purpose of the final question is not to criticize a particular style of worship but to examine our own attitudes and actions in worship. Do we sense that we stand together with other believers in the presence of our conquering King? Do we submit ourselves fully to him and to his Word in our worship? Are we casually comfortable or waiting in hopeful anticipation for the arrival of the King of glory?

Study 8. The Clouds of Heaven. Daniel 7:9-14; Revelation 19:1-16.

Purpose: To stir our hearts to joyful anticipation of Jesus' return.

Question 1. You may want to take a *Pictionary* approach to this question. As you talk about each element in the vision, have a different group member add it to the composite picture and then discuss what that element communicates to you about the character and power of the heavenly being. The person seen by Daniel can only be God, but Daniel only sees a visual representation of God. This isn't what God looks like since God the Father has no body or hair or clothes (see Jn 1:18). God is pure spirit (Jn 4:24). The representation Daniel sees is designed to convey aspects of what the invisible God is like.

The whiteness of God's robe portrays his purity and truthfulness. The whiteness of his hair pictures maturity and wisdom. Along with the title "Ancient of Days," white hair also marks God out as an eternal being. The throne of God is able to move, showing God's universal authority to bring judgment, and the fire denotes his holy ability to judge evil thoroughly and completely. The number of God's attendants, holy angels, picture God's majesty and sovereign authority to carry out whatever he determines to do. The courtroom of God's justice was prepared and ready to bring down the powers of evil and injustice on the earth. (See Leon Wood, *A Commentary on Daniel* [Grand Rapids: Zondervan, 1973], pp. 188-90.)

Question 2. All human authority will someday be swept away by God's direct intervention in human history. Cruel tyrants (like the "beast" and the "horn" in Daniel's vision) are certain to fall under the all-encompassing judgment of God, but even civil, democratic governments can be riddled with injustice and corruption. Only when the right ruler sits on the throne of God's kingdom will justice and righteousness prevail.

Question 3. The "son of man" in this vision is human, but he arrives on the scene on the clouds of heaven. He is ushered directly into the presence of Almighty God without hesitation and he receives glory and sovereign power directly from God's hand. He also receives worship that belongs to God alone. The son of man's kingdom does not last just through two presidential terms or even through a human lifetime; his dominion is everlasting and will never weaken or fall to an outside conqueror.

Question 4. Christians are certainly called to seek justice and peace in our present world, but we also realize that all human governments and leaders are imperfect. While we work against evil and oppression, we also have the confidence that God will one day bring his perfect justice to bear on those who are wicked and corrupt. They may seem to escape justice now, but they won't escape forever.

Question 5. The "shouts" in this chapter all originate in heaven. These are the words of angels and redeemed believers in heaven as they see God's great plan of redemption come to its climax in the return of Jesus to earth in power and glory. God is pictured as the sovereign King bringing judgment on the wicked and deliverance to the righteous. All his servants in heaven rejoice because the time of the wedding of the Lamb to his bride has finally come. You may want to read this passage as the narrator with the group members reading (or shouting!) the five expressions of praise.

Question 6. Group members may see themselves in more than one place in the passage. Any who see themselves as being struck down under God's wrath should be encouraged to seek or to rest in God's grace and forgiveness through faith in Jesus.

Question 7. No matter what trials or opposition or persecution we face today as Christians, we know how the story ends. Jesus will overcome—and we are in his hands.

Question 8. Several descriptive titles are given to Jesus in these verses—"Faithful and True," the "Word of God," "King of kings and Lord of lords." All the titles are designed to remind us of his future victory and ultimate triumph over every enemy. If you have time, encourage the group members to use the title that gives them the most confidence to address Jesus in prayer or in an expression of praise.

Douglas Connelly is senior pastor at Parkside Community Church in Sterling Heights, Michigan. A writer and speaker, Connelly has written many Bible study guides, including Good & Evil, Miracles, Following Jesus *and* Heroes of Faith, *all in the LifeGuide Bible Study Series.*

LifeGuide® in Depth Bible Studies

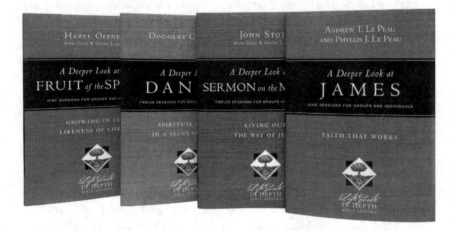

LifeGuide® in Depth Bible Studies help you to dive into the riches of Scripture by taking you further into themes and books than you might have gone before. As you see new connections between the Old and New Testament, gain an understanding of the historical and cultural background of passages, engage in creative exercises, and concretely apply what you've learned, you'll be amazed at the breadth of the knowledge and wisdom you gain and the transformation God can work in you as you meet him in his Word. Each session provides enough material for a week's worth of personal Scripture study along with a weekly group discussion guide that pulls all of the elements together.

These guides are based on and include the inductive Bible studies from the bestselling Life-Guide® Bible Study Series with over ten million copies sold. But they've been expanded for a new kind of study experience.